My Dear Teen Self:
A guided journal to help teens explore feelings and social scenarios

Jaynay Chanel Johnson

My Dear Teen Self

For more information contact: www.teentherapytalk.com

Book Cover Design by Nia E. Designs

Illustrations by Kay-Solo Designs

Photography by Floyd Shade

ISBN: 978-0-9989576-0-9
First Edition 2017109 8 7 6 5 4 3 21

"Journaling helped me release my thoughts in a safe way. My journal was there when no one was there to listen"

~Jaynay C. Johnson

Introduction:

I am overwhelmed with joy as I am writing this because it means I have completed my second book. This journal should be used as a tool to help you explore your thoughts and some of the challenges you may be experiencing. My teen years were not easy and I am grateful to be here to discuss those years with my writing. I want you to know all your dreams can be a reality. Life may start rocky, but you have the chance to change that. This journal is your personal safe space. Write your deepest feelings and thoughts in here. After all, life is about learning, growing and feeling

~Jaynay C. Johnson

Instructions:

This is a guided journal with prompts to help you think about feelings, issues and situations that you may face while being a teenager. Be sure to answer each statement and question honestly.

1. What do I expect of my life?

2. How will I be able to achieve that expectation?

3. Does my family support me?

4. If they do not, explore how you may be able to overcome that barrier.

5. If your family supports you, what about their support helps you through?

6. Do you feel you need more support?

Positive Me Challenge

WRITE 10 THINGS THAT YOU LIKE ABOUT YOURSELF

7. How does social media impact your life?

8. Do you find yourself doing things for likes or follows?

9. How far would you go to get likes or follows?

10. Do you get pressured to do things by your friends?

I AM THE
BEST EDITION
OF MYSELF

Build A Friend Activity
FROM THIS LIST OF QUALITIES, BUILD YOUR IDEAL FRIEND

FRIEND QUALITIES BANK

Loyal- Dependable- Possessive
Understanding – Deceitful
Aggressive – Sincere –
Thoughtful- Honest – Forgiving
Unadventurous – Optimistic
Obedient – Moralistic – Friendly
Intelligent– Ambitious – Nice
Popular – Creative – Confident
Respectful

My Ideal Friend is...

[   ]

11. What do your friends typically pressure you to do?

12. Are you more loyal to your friends than they are to you?

13. How frequently are you checking in with yourself about how you feel?

14. What is the feeling that you get most in a day?

15. Write out why you may be experiencing that feeling so much.

16. Is that feeling overwhelming? How do you cope?

Draw...

WHERE YOU TYPICALLY FEEL ANGER, SADNESS, HAPPINESS, FEAR AND OTHER EMOTIONS YOU MAY FEEL. CHOOSE A COLOR TO CORRESPOND WITH EACH FEELING.

17. Define coping skills.
Use Google if you need to.

18. Tell me what your coping
skills are.

19. Do you have thoughts of not wanting to be here?

20. If you weren't, what would be different for you?

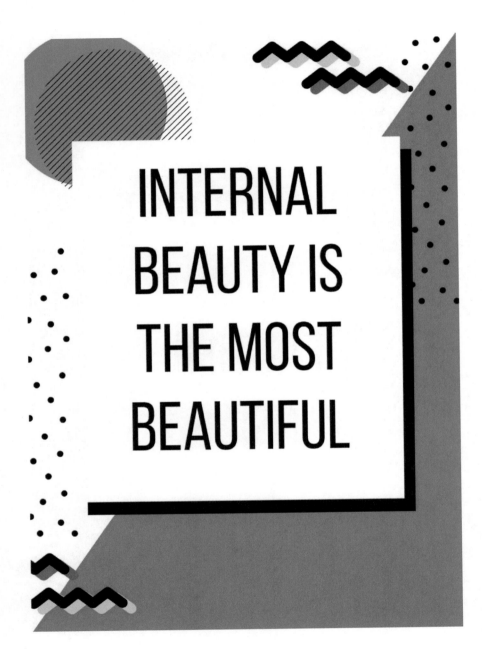

INTERNAL BEAUTY IS THE MOST BEAUTIFUL

21. Share 3 things that would make your life better.

22. Define self-esteem.

23. On first thought, do you have high or low self-esteem?

24. What helped to shape your self-esteem?

self love

WRITE WHAT YOU LOVE ABOUT YOURSELF

self love

WRITE WHAT YOU LOVE ABOUT YOURSELF

25. Define "Bully".

26. Have you ever been or are you currently a bully? This includes on social media.

27. If so, how do you think you became one?

28. How do you think you can stop?

29. Is someone not liking you make them a hater?

30. Name 5 places you want to visit and why.

31. If there's one issue in the world that you had the power to fix, what would it be?

32. As a teen, what do you need more of?

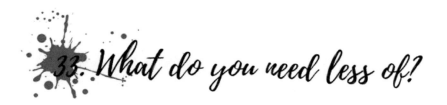

33. What do you need less of?

BE BOLD,
AMBITIOUS &
CREATIVE

34. Talk about your relationship with your mother.

35. Talk about your relationship with your father.

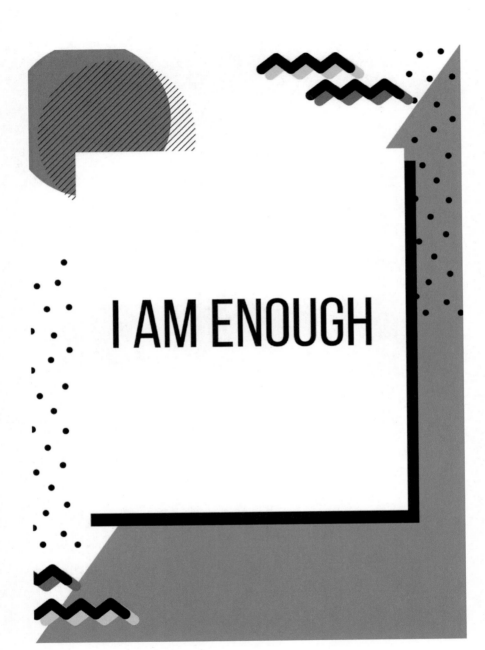

I AM ENOUGH

DARE
TO
BEGIN

36. Discuss/describe what you wish those relationships were like.

37. What is the rest of your family like?

Circle of Trust
WHO'S IN YOUR CIRCLE OF TRUST?
WRITE DOWN THE PEOPLE YOU TRUST CURRENTLY.

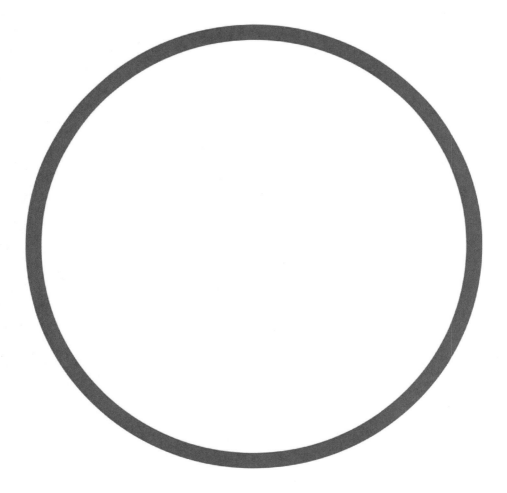

38.What type of friend are you?

39. What type of friends do you have?

40. Are you heavily influenced by your friends and peers?

47. Do you use your friends as replacement for family?

42. In a romantic relationship, do you know what you bring to the table?

43. What are your values as a person?

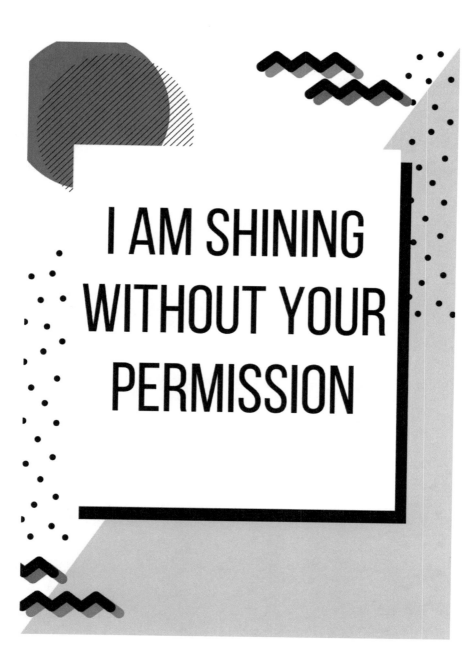

I AM GIFTED WITH TALENT THAT ONLY I POSSESS

44. Do you feel loved?

45. Define/describe love that comes from a parent.

46. Define/describe love that comes from a romantic partner.

47. Define/describe love that comes from a romantic friend.

Love Heart!

WRITE THINGS AND PEOPLE THAT YOU LOVE INSIDE THE HEART BELOW. IN SMALLER HEARTS, WRITE NAMES OF THE PEOPLE THAT YOU WANT TO LOVE YOU.

48. Are you sexually active?

49. Does sex add value to your life? How so?

50. Are you having sex for yourself or were your pressured?

51. Do you understand sex beyond the act?

52. What does sex mean to you?

53. How are babies created?

54. What is a menstrual cycle?

Female Reproductive System

LABEL PARTS OF THE FEMALE REPRODUCTIVE SYSTEM USING THE WORD BANK BELOW

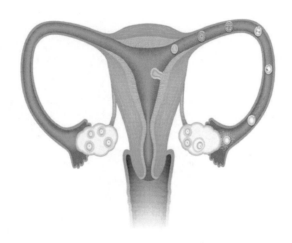

Cervix

Ovary **UTERUS**

Vagina **Fallopian Tubes**

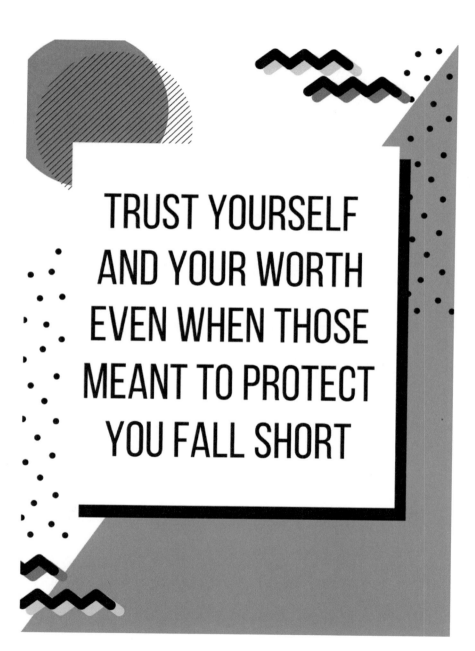

TRUST YOURSELF AND YOUR WORTH EVEN WHEN THOSE MEANT TO PROTECT YOU FALL SHORT

THE SUN IS ALWAYS SHINING BEHIND THE CLOUDS

55. List people you are comfortable talking to:

56. Where do you feel the safest?

57. How do you define yourself?

58. How do you think others define you?

59. Create a name acronym for yourself. *Example: Jane – Jolly, Ambitious, Neutral, Exciting*

60. What is the definition of loyalty?

61. Do you focus more on loyalty in relationships than anything else? If so, why?

62. Define mental health and share any experiences you have had with it.

63. Nightmares, are they happening often? What is happening in your nightmares?

64. What do you often dream about?

65. What do you need to be forgiven for?

66. Whom do you need to forgive?

LOVE
YOURSELF
INFINITELY

67. If you could go back in time anywhere and "any when" where/when would you go and why?

68. Begin a list of questions that you would like to have answered. They may be about the future or the past.

69. What do you consider your greatest accomplishment to date and why?

70. Write about disappointment.

71. Write about who you will be in 10 years and 20 years from now.

72. Describe a fight you had with your mother. Now, tell it from her point of view.

73. Describe a fight you had with your father. Now, tell it from his point of view.

THE SKY'S THE LIMIT

74. Write about things that your family has taught you.

75. Describe a happy memory of your family.

76. Write about some of the things that you worry about.

77. Describe the one thing that gives you the most comfort.

THIS SECTION WILL HELP YOU
EXPLORE SOCIAL SCENARIOS

Instructions

THIS PART OF THE JOURNAL
IS ABOUT SOCIAL SCENARIOS YOU MAY FIND
YOURSELF DEALING WITH. SHARE HOW YOU
COULD POTENTIALLY HANDLE THIS SITUATION
IF IT WERE TO HAPPEN TO YOU.

Vignette

You and your friend Kim were invited to Tyrone's house to watch a movie with his friend. They begin to touch you and you are not comfortable with it, however, your friend Kim likes it. What could you do?

You are taking a test and the guy behind you asks you for help. You think he is cute and you like him. He wants to know what you put for question number two. What could you do?

Vignette

Your friends came over to your house for a "get together." One of your friends brought another friend and posted it on Snapchat, so now there are more people there. They bring drinks & drugs. What could you do?

Vignette

You are out at the mall with your friends and you see a shirt you love. Your friend encourages you to steal it since you do not have the money. They take something to show you it is easy to get away with. What could you do?

Vignette 5

Someone sends you a nude photo of one of your
peers. You save it. A few days later, you hear that she
was talking about you. Your friend tells you to post
her nude picture. What could you do?

Your mom has a new boyfriend and he drinks a lot. He constantly says inappropriate things to you when she is not around. This makes you uncomfortable. What could you do?

A peer threatened to beat you up after school and you are on your last strike at school. The principal told you one more fight and you would be expelled. What could you do?

Your friend goes missing after a party you were at with them. You are afraid you will get in trouble for being at the party, but you have an idea what happened. What could you do?

Your partner abuses you and tells you if you tell anyone they will hurt your younger siblings that are often with you. What could you do?

You and your partner were engaging in sexual activity and he recorded you with your permission. He sent the video to everyone in the school. How could you handle this situation?

Suggestions for Vignettes

- Identify a trusted adult in your life that can help you navigate situations.
- Take some time to think through a situation once it is presented to you.
- Do not feel pressured to say yes to everything suggested to you.
- Create an exit strategy for yourself in every setting.
- Include your parents in your life; even you are scared you will get in trouble. They will want to make sure you are SAFE first.
- Use your social media to alert people if you are in an unsafe situation.
- If you are being bullied talk to an adult you trust and talk to your parents.
- If you are not able to talk to a parent about an issue or the problem is your parent, tell an adult at your school such as a teacher, school counselor, or nurse.
- Do not be afraid to say no.
- Find an activity to engage in which will consume your time. When you have an activity, sport or hobby, you may find you have less time to just "hangout."

Pledge: RECITE & SIGN

Dear Teen Self,

I love you! You are unique and beautiful in many ways. You never have to apologize for being yourself. You do need to choose to heal on purpose and make positive choices. I am in control of my happiness. Girl, you are amazing and you will make it.

Love,

_____

Signature

Shh!
THOUGHTS LOADING.....

Dear Teen Self...

Dear Teen Self...

Be sure to stay in touch with us!

Instagram @dearteenself

Facebook @dearteenself

Website:www.teentherapytalk.com

Email: info@dearteenself.com

Hashtags

#dearteenself #mydearteenselfjournal
#DearJournal

ABOUT THE AUTHOR

Jaynay C. Johnson is a published writer, teen therapist, speaker, and parent coach. She is author of Dear Teen Self: Tips to help teenage girls navigate through adolescence.

Jaynay teaches teen emotional health techniques to a wide variety of audiences. She has developed tools to help teenagers and parents strengthen their bond through numerous mediums. Similarly, she consults with other clinicians that are looking to strengthen their understanding of working with teenagers.

Please visit www.teentherapytalk.com for more information.

Made in the USA
Middletown, DE
19 March 2019